GREAT BRITONS

SPORTING
HEROES

Moira Butterfield

FRANKLIN WATTS
LONDON • SYDNEY

First published in 2007 by
Franklin Watts

Copyright © Franklin
Watts 2007

Franklin Watts
338 Euston Road
London NW1 3BH

Franklin Watts Australia
Level 17/207 Kent Street
Sydney, NSW 2000

A CIP catalogue record for
this book is available from
the British Library.

Dewey number: 796.08

ISBN: 978 0 7496 7474 8

Printed in China

Franklin Watts is a division
of Hachette Children's
Books, an Hachette Livre
UK company.

Designer: Thomas Keenes
Art Director: Jonathan Hair
Editor: Sarah Ridley
Editor-in-Chief:
John C. Miles
Picture Research:
Diana Morris

Picture credits:
AP/Topham: 35. Empics/PA
Photos: 9, 19, 30. Harry
How/Getty Images: 37.
Hulton Archive/Getty
Images: 10. Piers
Macdonald/Topfoto: 33.
PA/Topfoto: 25, 29, 38, 41,
43. Picturepoint/Topham:
13, 20. Prosport/Topfoto:
cover, 27. UPP/Topfoto: 16.
Topfoto: 7, 15, 23. Alex
Woods/Topfoto: 45.

Every attempt has been
made to clear copyright.
Should there be any
inadvertent omission
please apply to the
publisher for rectification.

CONTENTS

INTRODUCTION

The 21 sportspeople in this book are all champions and record-breakers. Many of them have been given honours, such as medals and knighthoods, for their contribution to British sporting life. They have all given sports fans great excitement and pleasure watching their performances, and they are all famous household names. Some are still world-renowned many decades after their careers, because they made such a big impact on the public.

All the sportspeople we have chosen have not only achieved much for themselves, but they have helped make their chosen sport more popular. They have also inspired young sportspeople to copy their winning example. Those that are still alive often use their fame to raise money for charity and many give advice to young competitors following in their footsteps.

In the time period covered by this book, big changes have come about in sport. The first sportspeople mentioned performed when it was frowned on, and often illegal, to be a 'professional' – making money from sport. Gradually that attitude has changed and now successful sportspeople can earn a great deal, not just from performing, but from endorsements – letting their name be used to advertise something.

Another big difference is in training and equipment. Hi-tech science is now used to make sure sportspeople perform to the very best of their ability. The third big change is that modern sportspeople are treated as celebrities, with newspapers reporting all there is to know about their lives.

There are many British sporting heroes and heroines who could not be included in this book. We have chosen just a small selection, from different sports and with different stories to tell. It's fun to make a list of your top 20 sporting favourites, deciding who should go in and why. Try it with your sports-loving friends and see if you can agree!

WG GRACE
FIRST FAMOUS CRICKETER

BORN Downend, Bristol, 18 July 1848
DIED London, 23 October 1915
AGE 67 years

WG Grace was a sporting celebrity in the late 19th century and was said to be better known than British royalty at the time. He made cricket the most popular spectator sport of its day, and he is still recognised as one of England's greatest sporting heroes.

William Gilbert Grace played cricket from a young age with his three cricket-mad brothers. His first competitive match was at the age of nine, and at the age of 15 he was good enough to play for an All-England team. After school, he trained to become a doctor (GP) and ran a surgery in Bristol, though he was rarely there during the cricket season.

'Professional' sportsmen, who made a living only from sport, were frowned on at the time. All his life Grace played officially as an 'amateur', even though he demanded high fees for appearing and made a fortune from the game. When he was playing, admission fees to cricket matches doubled because he was so entertaining and he expected to be paid well for his appearances. He was the first British sportsman to make a great deal of money from his talent.

During a 44-year career, Grace scored an amazing 54,896 first class runs, which

The 'Glorious Amateur'

Professional sportsmen were looked down on as 'ungentlemanly' for many years in Britain. Players were meant to play for the love of the game, and not for money. An example of a true 'gentleman' amateur was **CHARLES BURGESS (CB) FRY** (1872–1956). Not only was he a famous cricketer but also a world record-holding athlete, rugby player and international footballer, who never played sport for money. He was also in politics and was once offered the throne of Albania. While WG Grace is still a controversial figure in cricket because of his attitudes to money, CB Fry is often held up as a model sportsman.

WG Grace takes guard, ready to add to his run total and his fame as an early sporting hero.

was particularly impressive because in those days pitches were poor and high scores were difficult to make. His highest score was 400 not out, and he made ten double-centuries (200 runs). Once he batted for a double century over two days whilst sitting up with a patient all night in between. He was also a good bowler, and took 2,876 wickets. He was not a polite sportsman, being well-known for arguing with umpires and trying to put players off by talking, or by shouting at them. His 'win at any price' attitude was shocking to many, but made him a big hit with the public.

The crowds flocked to see Grace, whose nickname was 'The Doctor'. He was instantly recognisable because of his big build and his long, bushy beard. He had massive wide shoulders and, in later life, he grew too fat to field. He made such an impression during his career that he is still world-famous today.

ARTHUR WHARTON
FIRST ENGLISH BLACK FOOTBALLER

BORN Ghana, West Africa, 28 October 1865
DIED Balby, Doncaster, 12 December 1930
AGE 65 years

Over a century ago, Arthur Wharton was England's first black professional footballer. His ground-breaking achievement was forgotten and only rediscovered in the 1990s. Now he is an inspiration to modern black footballers.

Wharton was born in Ghana. His father was a missionary from Grenada in the West Indies, and his mother was connected to the Ghanaian royal family. In 1884, when he was 19, Wharton came to England to train as a Methodist minister (priest). While he was at college he played cricket and set a cycling record. Then, in 1886, he became the fastest man in Britain when he won a national 100-yard running race in 10 seconds. He decided to become a professional athlete instead of a minister, and his all-round sporting talent was spotted by Darlington Football Club. Until 1885, when professionalism was first made legal in the game, football was only played by amateurs (players who were not paid a wage). There was no League Championship at the time although there was the FA Cup. Instead there were local competitions and county matches.

International pioneer

ANDREW WATSON (1857–date unknown) was Britain's first black international footballer, and, as far as we know, the world's first ever black football administrator. He was born in British Guiana, and is thought to have begun his career in Scottish football around 1874, predating Wharton's English debut.

He played for Queen's Park, Glasgow, and for Scotland, where he was equally good in defence or midfield. He went on to become Queen's Park Club Secretary, one of the first and only black people ever to make it onto the governing board of a British football team.

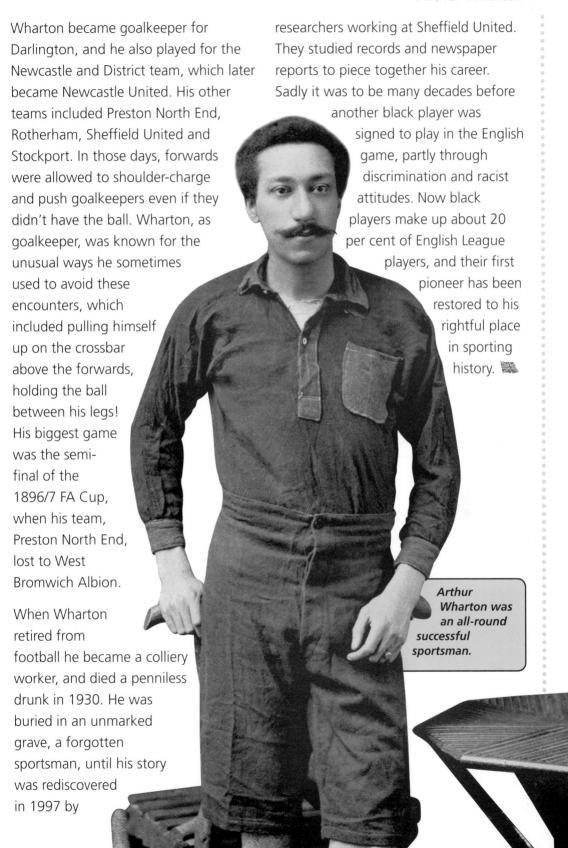

Wharton became goalkeeper for Darlington, and he also played for the Newcastle and District team, which later became Newcastle United. His other teams included Preston North End, Rotherham, Sheffield United and Stockport. In those days, forwards were allowed to shoulder-charge and push goalkeepers even if they didn't have the ball. Wharton, as goalkeeper, was known for the unusual ways he sometimes used to avoid these encounters, which included pulling himself up on the crossbar above the forwards, holding the ball between his legs! His biggest game was the semi-final of the 1896/7 FA Cup, when his team, Preston North End, lost to West Bromwich Albion.

When Wharton retired from football he became a colliery worker, and died a penniless drunk in 1930. He was buried in an unmarked grave, a forgotten sportsman, until his story was rediscovered in 1997 by researchers working at Sheffield United. They studied records and newspaper reports to piece together his career. Sadly it was to be many decades before another black player was signed to play in the English game, partly through discrimination and racist attitudes. Now black players make up about 20 per cent of English League players, and their first pioneer has been restored to his rightful place in sporting history. 🇬🇧

Arthur Wharton was an all-round successful sportsman.

KATHLEEN 'KITTY' GODFREE

FIRST WOMAN SPORTS STAR

BORN Scotland, 7 May 1896
DIED London, 19 June 1992
AGE 96 years

Kitty Godfree (born Kathleen McKane) made tennis popular throughout the nation in the 1920s, and paved the way for women to achieve sporting fame.

Kitty Godfree in the tennis costume of the time, considered daring and modern.

Kitty won the women's singles at the Wimbledon Lawn Tennis Championship twice and also won an amazing five Olympic tennis medals at the 1920 and 1924 Olympics, a record that still stands as the best British woman's medal tally. Altogether she won 146 matches at Wimbledon. In addition, in 1926 she won the mixed doubles with her tennis-playing husband Leslie, the only married couple ever to do so. She didn't stop at tennis, and was four times British badminton champion.

Along with other players of her era, Kitty helped bring about big changes in tennis. She and her co-players wore fashionable headbands and loose knee-length dresses (which were considered shockingly revealing), instead of the long dresses and corsets worn by earlier players. In the 1920s tennis players began to serve overarm, not underam, and Kitty was one of the first women to use volleys in her game.

Unlike modern professionals she didn't get hours of training from a coach, and was a self-taught player. Her greatest strengths were her guts and tenacity. When she won her title in 1924, she came back from 4-1 games down. Her prize for winning was a great deal less than players receive today, and players had to be amateur. In 1926 Kitty's Wimbledon title prize was a £5 token for a London department store.

Kitty remained an inspiration to players, and played all her life. In 1988 she played in a tennis international club match against France, aged 92. She was treated as an honoured guest at Wimbledon and presented the trophy to Martina Navratilova in 1986, to mark a 100 years of women's Wimbledon tennis. Kitty was one of the first sportswomen ever to become famous through newspaper photos and press coverage, and her fame lasted throughout her life.

Tennis champions of the future

Nowadays tennis is a much more international competition, with players from many countries competing for top titles, such as the Wimbledon Championship. Only a few Britons have become Wimbledon champions since Kitty's time, including **FRED PERRY** (1909–96) and **VIRGINIA WADE** (1945–). Young players, such as Scotland's **ANDREW MURRAY** (1987–), must work day in, day out, at their fitness and technique to succeed in the modern game, but in return the prize money is far, far bigger than in Kitty's day.

SIR ROGER BANNISTER
FIRST RUNNER TO BREAK THE 4-MINUTE MILE

BORN Harrow, 23 March 1929

On May 6th, 1954, the news flashed around the world that Roger Bannister had become the first athlete ever to run a mile officially in under four minutes. Bannister shot to worldwide fame – celebrity which has lasted all his life.

Bannister was a good runner at school but spent most of his time studying as he wanted to go to university and become a doctor. This he achieved, fitting in running when he could.

In 1954, like all athletes at the time, Bannister was a strictly amateur runner, meaning he was not allowed to earn money from running. He was inspired to improve after he ran disappointingly in the 1952 Olympics. He realised that the winning runners were doing carefully-planned intensive training and he decided to try the same techniques. He was one of the first athletes to understand modern sports psychology, too. He knew that the ability to win was 'in the head' as well as being physical.

Bannister's big rival at the time, Australian runner John Landy, was intending to make a record attempt, so Bannister decided to try first and planned a race at the Ifley Road track in Oxford. The day he chose turned out to be so blustery he almost called the race off, but decided to go ahead at the last minute. He was helped by two pacemakers, running to help him keep his speed up. They were Chris Brasher and Chris Chataway, and they became world-famous, too, for taking part. Nerves told at the start when Brasher made a false start. The race began at the second attempt and Brasher ran at the front. Bannister shouted, 'Faster, faster!' to his colleagues as he ran sandwiched between them. Then Chataway took

British track success

Britain has had many fine middle-distance athletes since Roger Bannister. Great middle-distance running names include Olympic gold-medal winners **SEBASTIAN COE** (1956–), **STEVE OVETT** (1955–) and **STEVE CRAM** (1960–). All three broke records and won many world-class races. ('Middle-distance' means the 800m, 1500m and 3000m races. A mile is just over 1500m.)

Exhaustion shows on the face of Roger Bannister after his record-breaking run.

over at the front before Bannister sprinted ahead over the last 250 yards. The watching crowd went wild when his time of 3 minutes and 59.4 seconds was announced. The following month John Landy smashed the record, but Bannister will always be remembered as the first to break the mile. Bannister retired as an athlete in 1954 and concentrated on his career as a doctor. Nowadays highly-trained professional athletes break the 4-minute mile fairly regularly but they have far more training, much better-quality running tracks and better weather conditions than Roger Bannister experienced. His record-breaking run still stands out as a mighty achievement. He was knighted by Queen Elizabeth II in 1975 for services to sport. 🇬🇧

SIR STIRLING MOSS
GREAT BRITISH RACING DRIVER

BORN London,
17 September 1929

Stirling Moss became a world-famous racing driver in the 1950s. Although he never won a World Championship, he had a remarkable racing career in many different types of car and became the most well-known name in motorsport.

Both of Stirling Moss's parents competed in motor racing, and at the age of nine his father bought him an old car that he was allowed to drive around the fields surrounding his home. He won his first car race aged 18, got his first Formula One Grand Prix win at the British Grand Prix in 1955, and went on to win 16 Grand Prix races altogether. Three times he was runner-up in the World Championship, though he never won it.

Moss became our most famous racing driver, and made Formula One very popular in the UK. It was seen as a glamorous sport, and he contributed to the image by becoming the highest-paid driver in the world. Recognisable by his trademark white helmet, he was a stylish racer who always raised his hand in acknowledgement as he passed someone in an impressive car such as a Maserati or an Aston Martin. He was ahead of his time in making

A glamorous but deadly sport

Britain had a number of successful racing drivers in the 1950s and 60s. In those days, racing cars were much less strongly built than they are now, and the race tracks were much less safe than they are today. This meant that a race crash was much more likely to be fatal. Talented British driver **JIM CLARKE** (1936–68) died during a race, along with a number of other drivers of that era, and Stirling Moss was lucky to survive his terrible accident.

business deals, signing up to endorse products in a way that modern sportspeople find normal but in his day was unusual.

As well as Formula One, Moss seemed able to turn his hand to any kind of driving, and still win. Altogether he competed in 84 different types of cars in his career, and did well with them all. But in 1962 he had a head-on crash that put him in a coma and paralysed one side of his body. Although he recovered, he realised his reactions were not as sharp as they had been and he decided not to race regularly again. However, he has never stopped driving and still competes in exhibition races in historic cars. In 1999 he was knighted for his services to British sport. Though he never won a World Championship, he is one of the best-known sportsmen this country has produced. 🇬🇧

Stirling Moss holds his famous white helmet after winning yet another motor race.

SIR JACKIE STEWART
FORMULA ONE CHAMPION

BORN Dumbartonshire, Scotland, 11 June 1939

Jackie Stewart was three times Formula One World Champion, and campaigned to make racing safer for drivers. In the late 1960s and early 1970s he was Britain's most successful racing star.

Jackie Stewart is one of Scotland's most famous and successful sporting heroes.

When Jackie Stewart left school, he went to work in his father's garage. He almost made the UK Olympic shooting team before he decided to take up motor racing instead. In his first season in Formula One he came third in the Championship behind two other Britons, Jim Clarke and Graham Hill. He went on to win the Championship three times and finished second twice. His most amazing win was probably in the 1968 German Grand Prix, when he drove to victory through mist and pouring rain while suffering from a broken wrist. He was always recognisable in his car because he wore a tartan racing helmet.

Eight years later, on the eve of his 100th race, Stewart decided to retire. Upset by the death of his good friend Francois Cevert in a qualifying race, he felt it was time for him to end his career. During his time as a driver, and afterwards, he campaigned to make racing safer for drivers. He himself nearly died in the 1966 Belgian Grand Prix, when a crash left him trapped in his car covered in petrol. The lack of medical care he got that day, and the death of several drivers he knew well, made him determined to try to change the sport. Partly thanks to Stewart, racing drivers today receive top-quality medical attention and race tracks are lined with crash barriers to prevent drivers hitting trees and spectators.

After he gave up driving, Stewart

British drivers rule!

British drivers have had much success in different types of motor racing. **GRAHAM HILL** (1929–75) and **JAMES HUNT** (1947–93) were both World Champions, heroes who brought great glamour to the sport. **NIGEL MANSELL** (1953–) and **DAMON HILL** (1960–) both became World Formula One champions, and **COLIN McRAE** (1968–) became the first British World Rally Champion. Young drivers such as **JENSON BUTTON** (1980–) and **LEWIS HAMILTON** (1985–) are set to keep up the country's record of success.

became a commentator, was knighted, and ran his own racing team for a while. The team won one Grand Prix, which he said was his proudest moment ever. Eventually he sold the team to Ford for a reputed $100 million dollars.

Jackie Stewart is dyslexic but, although it held him back at school, it hasn't prevented him from becoming a top sportsman and a very rich businessman, too. Nowadays he campaigns to help get the problem of dyslexia recognised early, so that dyslexic schoolchildren can receive the help they need to succeed. 🇬🇧

BOBBY MOORE OBE
FOOTBALL WORLD CUP WINNER

BORN Barking, Essex, 12 April 1941
DIED London, 24 February 1993
AGE 51 years

Bobby Moore captained England to their one and only World Cup win in 1966, and is widely regarded as one of the best defenders who ever played.

Moore began his playing career as a schoolboy at West Ham. He got into the England team in 1962, and wore the number 6 shirt for over ten years and 108 England matches. He was a superb tackler and could read the game – working out what was about to happen on the pitch. He had great passing and positioning skills, too. High praise came from Brazilian superstar Pelé, who said that Moore was the best defender he ever played against. Moore's reputation on and off the field for gentlemanly behaviour made him an ideal captain, whom everyone respected.

In the 1966 World Cup, England's solid defence, directed by Moore, did not concede a goal until the semi-final. In the final, England went 1–0 down to West Germany but Moore took a quick free kick, enabling striker Geoff Hurst to score an equaliser. Martin Peters scored again for England; then West Germany scored in the last few minutes and forced the match into extra time. Geoff Hurst scored two in extra time, making the final result England 4, West Germany 2. Bobby Moore went up to receive the Cup from the Queen. A famous piece of TV footage shows Bobby trying hard to wipe as much mud off his hands as he could before meeting her, showing the whole world what a polite and good-mannered man he was.

Moore's list of achievements include European and FA Cup-winning medals, and Player of the Year awards. He

World Cup lost and found

In 1966 the World Cup was held in Britain. Disaster struck before the tournament when the solid gold £30,000 Jules Rimet trophy was stolen from an exhibition in London. It was found a week later by a mongrel dog called Pickles, out for a walk with his owner in South London. Pickles discovered it wrapped in newspaper in some bushes in Norwood, South London.

transferred from West Ham to Fulham in 1974, for what seemed like a lot of money at the time – £25,000. He then played in the USA before retiring as a player in 1978.

Moore tried football management and then TV commentating. Unfortunately, he was diagnosed with bowel cancer and died just a few days after his last commentary. His ashes were scattered in the City of London cemetery, where they now fly an England flag whenever England play a match.

West Ham Football Club have a stand named after their most famous player and his bronze statue is going to stand at the entrance to the new Wembley Stadium, a monument to one of the best players England ever produced.

Bobby Moore playing for Fulham against West Ham in the FA Cup final on 3 May 1975.

GEORGE BEST
FIRST CELEBRITY FOOTBALLER

BORN Belfast, 22 May 1946
DIED London, 25 November 2005
AGE 59 years

George Best was the first celebrity footballer to be as famous for his lifestyle as for his football. He had dazzling skills as a striker for Manchester United, alongside a troubled life of alcoholism and bad behaviour.

George Best (far left) was identified with 1960s style and became a real celebrity.

Sport and celebrity

Nowadays famous sportspeople in Britain are just as likely to have their private lives reported in the newspapers as their sporting careers. Help and advice is now available to them on coping with the pressure, something that was not on hand for George Best in the 1960s when no sportsperson had ever before been treated like a popstar. Even in today's highly-professional sports world, sportstars sometimes let their superstar status get in the way of their sporting performance. Then their lifestyle is as likely to get them in the news as their sports ability.

As a Belfast schoolboy, George Best was spotted by a Manchester United scout, who sent a telegram to Manchester United manager Matt Busby, reading: 'I think I've found you a genius.' He was signed as a professional footballer by Manchester United when he was 17, and at 18 he began to play for Northern Ireland, too. In his heyday at Manchester United he won European and League medals alongside other famous footballers of the time, Bobby Charlton and Denis Law. He was famed for his lightning speed and his ability to use either foot to weave the ball past a defence player. His deftly-timed movements around other players made him look almost like a dancer.

Because of Best's good looks and liking for parties, he made the newspaper headlines. He was nicknamed the 'Fifth Beatle' because he was as famous as the Beatles pop group in the 1960s. He lived the life of a champagne-drinking playboy and was constantly followed by the press, who put his complicated lovelife on the front pages. It was the first time this had ever happened to a sportsman, and Best found the pressure hard to handle. He became an alcoholic and finally left Manchester United under a cloud in 1974, after repeatedly failing to turn up for training. He played for Fulham and in the United States for a while, before giving up football. Best did not give up his drinking habit and partying, and eventually this led to bankruptcy, a prison sentence and a liver transplant. He was regularly in the news right up until his premature death in 2005. There are lots of famous quotes from him on his lifestyle, such as: 'I spent all my money on booze, women and fast cars. The rest I wasted.'

Over 100,000 people lined the streets of Belfast for his funeral, and tributes came from footballers around the world, reminding everyone of his fantastic soccer skills rather than the personal problems that had dogged him for much of his life. Belfast Airport was renamed after him in 2006. 🇬🇧

GARETH EDWARDS MBE
LEGENDARY WELSH RUGBY PLAYER

BORN Swansea, Wales, 12th July 1947

The 1970s was a golden era for Welsh rugby, and its greatest star was Gareth Edwards. He scored what many think was the best try ever.

Edwards was a miner's son whose talent for rugby was first spotted by a teacher at his local school. He then won a sports scholarship to top English public school, Millfield. At the age of 19, he played his first rugby international for Wales. He played at scrum-half, and is said to have been the best ever. He could weave round a rugby defence, run at top speed, and he was clever and

strong, too. He used imagination when he played, thinking quickly to find ways to get round opposition players.

Edwards played 53 times between 1967 and 1978, and scored 20

The golden age of rugby

Welsh rugby players dominated the 1970s. The list included **BARRY JOHN** (1945–), nicknamed 'The King' and said to be the best fly-half in rugby history. He formed a fabulous partnership with Gareth Edwards, for Wales, and the British Lions. He was known for his devastating runs through the opposition defence. Rugby names such as his are still revered in Wales because the glorious victories of the 1970s lifted the spirits of the nation.

tries. He was Wales' youngest captain at the age of 20, and helped Wales to win five Triple Crowns (beating Ireland, Scotland and England), and three Grand Slams (beating the other nations and France as well). As a touring international he played for the British Lions, including the only team to win a series in New Zealand. He also played for the international team of top players, the Barbarians, for whom he scored what is often considered the greatest try ever on 27 January 1973, at Cardiff Arms Park against the New Zealand All Blacks. The ball began with Welsh teammate Phil Bennett, who

sidestepped the seemingly unbeatable New Zealanders and gave the ball to fellow Welshman JPR Williams. It passed through four more pairs of hands before Edwards ran with the ball and scored with a dive that will be remembered forever by many British rugby fans.

In 1978, at the height of his career, Edwards retired and came up against controversy when he accepted payment for his autobiography. He was said to have broken the amateur code of rugby then strictly in force. He was banned from coaching, but instead turned his hand to commentating, which he does both in English and in Welsh. His statue stands in Cardiff, a modern Welsh hero.

Gareth Edwards demonstrates his formidable rugby skills against Scotland in 1968.

BARRY SHEENE MBE
BRITISH MOTORCYCLE CHAMPION

BORN London,
11 September 1950
DIED Australia,
10 March 2003
AGE 52 years

Barry Sheene was a 1970s motorcycling World Champion who became a media star and brought motorcycle racing lots of new publicity. He is equally famous for recovering from serious race crashes.

Sheene had a motorbike mechanic father, and rode his first motorcycle at the age of five. After he left school, he raced motorcycles as much as possible, and managed to win the World 500cc Motorcycle Championship in 1976 and 1977. Overall he won many Grand Prix motorcycle races during his career. He rode for the Suzuki racing team and for Yamaha, and wore the number 7 on his bike and on his clothes.

Sheene's cheerful cockney character made him popular with the public, and he was often in the news for his glittering lifestyle. He was the first motorcycle rider to make money from endorsements (advertising). He often appeared on TV and even starred in a film and took part in an opera.

However, Sheene was also famous for recovering from serious motorcycle crashes. In 1975 he crashed at 175mph and was left with a broken thigh, a shattered arm, a broken collarbone and fractured ribs. Six weeks later he was back racing, and he went on to win the World Championship for Suzuki. Then, in 1982, another terrible crash left his legs smashed. They had to be rebuilt using metal plates and 28 screws.

Carl Fogarty, another great champion

CARL FOGARTY (1966–) is also a British motorcycle legend. He was four times World Superbike Champion from 1994 to 1999, for the Ducati racing team. Nicknamed 'Foggy', he was known for his highspeed cornering and his aggressive racing style. After a crash badly injured his shoulder, he retired in 2000 and set up his own superbike team. Champions such as Sheene and Fogarty still inspire young British motorcycle racers who hope to match their triumphs.

Barry Sheene MBE

Barry Sheene was a celebrity pin-up as well as an ace motorcycle racer.

Eventually Sheene retired from racing in 1985 but still occasionally rode in historic motorcycle races, usually beating everybody. His injuries left him suffering from arthritis and he moved to Australia because the warm climate helped with the pain. He became a commentator for Australian TV but sadly died from cancer in 2003. The Brands Hatch motorcycle track has a section called 'Sheene's Corner', named in his honour.

SIR IAN BOTHAM OBE
ENGLAND MATCH-WINNING CRICKETER

BORN Heswell, 24 November 1955

Ian Botham was a top England Test match cricketer from 1977 through to 1992. He was a match-winning entertainer on the pitch and a celebrity personality off it.

The young Botham was talented at football as well as cricket, but chose cricket and left school at 15 to play full-time for Somerset County Cricket Club. He soon made the England team for his all-round ability with the bat and ball. He had a never-say-die attitude and was able to pull his teams back from defeat with his gutsy performances. He was a fearless batsman who used his strength to score powerful sixes, and he was an accurate swing bowler who could make the ball move through the air away from and towards the wicket.

Altogether he played 103 Test matches for England, and broke lots of Test records. He scored 5,200 runs, took 383 wickets and 120 catches, and he hit several batting and bowling milestones in record time. His best international performance was for England against India in 1979/80, when he hit 114 and took 13 wickets. That made him the first Test player ever to score a century and take more than 10 wickets in one match. His legendary batting and bowling helped win England the Ashes in 1981, and the series was nicknamed 'Botham's Ashes'. In the same year he set a record of hitting six sixes in an England Test.

Botham was larger than life and had nicknames to match – 'Beefy' or 'Guy the Gorilla'. Sometimes he caused upset, falling out with team managers and cricket organisers. Scandals in his private

Cricket record-breakers

A group of young cricketers, partly inspired by Botham, are beginning to break some of his cricketing records. **ANDREW FLINTOFF** (1977–) broke Botham's record of hitting sixes when he hit nine of them during a match in 2005. **KEVIN PIETERSEN** (1980–) has also hit seven sixes in a match. Flintoff and Pietersen were both in the England team which regained the Ashes in 2005, for the first time since 1987. Botham's larger-than-life style of play has inspired future generations of young cricketers such as these.

Ian Botham shows the type of attacking shot for which he was famous.

life often made the papers, too. But many new fans began to follow cricket because of Botham, and though he is now retired he carries on notching up achievements in his life. He is now a commentator and appears on TV adverts. He has done several long-distance walks for charity and has raised over £5 million for causes such as Leukemia Research.

27

NICK FALDO MBE
BRITAIN'S GREATEST GOLFER

BORN Welwyn Garden City, 18 July 1957

Nick Faldo is one of Britain's most successful golfers, winning six major golf championships during his career. A golf legend, he remains involved in the sport.

Cycling was Faldo's best sport until the age of 13, when he saw a golf competition on television that included Jack Nicklaus. Inspired, he borrowed a set of clubs from a next-door neighbour and went to his local club to take some lessons. Four years later he was the best amateur player in Britain and he became a professional aged 19. After a few years he decided to work with a professional coach to teach himself to swing a golf club in a different way, so he could hit a better shot. It was a big gamble and it took a couple of years to pay off, but he went on to win six major golf championships between 1987 and 1996. Overall he won 42 golf titles and many millions in prize money. In 1992 he was the world's top golfer, both in results and earnings.

In 1977 Faldo became the youngest ever Ryder Cup player. The Ryder Cup is a golf competition played every two years between the USA and Europe. Faldo went on to become the most successful Ryder player of all time, winning more

points than anyone else. As an individual he was not an easy man to get on with, and sometimes upset people with his outspoken views, but in the Ryder Cup he proved that he could play well in a team. He was known as an incredibly hard-working golfer, always practising to improve his technique, even when he had already become a multi-millionaire golfing legend.

Nowadays Faldo is a TV commentator and golf course designer. He also helps young golfers in his coaching schools

Golf is British!

Britain has produced many fine golfers and it's not surprising because the competitive game of golf is said to have originated in Scotland. There were several ball and stick games played in medieval times, but the unique aim of Scottish golf was to use a stick to hit the ball into a hole in the ground. This idea spread throughout Britain and eventually the world.

and runs the Faldo Series competition for golfers aged between 11 and 21.

Nick Faldo holds the Claret Jug, the prize for winning the British Open Championship.

JANE TORVILL OBE AND CHRISTOPHER DEAN OBE
ICE-DANCING CHAMPIONS

JANE TORVILL:
BORN Nottingham,
7 October 1957
CHRISTOPHER DEAN:
BORN Nottingham,
27 July 1958

Jane Torvill and Christopher Dean are the most successful British ice-dancers ever. Their Winter Olympics gold medal-winning performance in 1984 was watched on TV by millions of Britons.

Torvill and Dean perform their passionate and dramatic ice-dance to Ravel's Bolero.

Jane Torvill got hooked on skating after a school trip to an ice-rink when she was eight years old. She became the British Pairs Champion aged 14. Christopher Dean took up skating at the age of ten, when he got a pair of skates as a Christmas present. Chris worked as a policeman in Nottingham and Jane worked as an insurance clerk, but both spent all their spare time competing in ice-dance, at first with different partners. An ice-dancing coach put them together as a team in 1975 and they won their first trophy in 1976. They came fifth in the Winter Olympics of 1980. Now a grant from the local council gave them enough money to give up their jobs and skate full-time.

They began to win regularly, and developed a new style of theatrical dance routine. Instead of dancing to several different snippets of music in one performance, as skaters normally did, they used one long piece of music and tried to act out a dramatic story to it while doing all the technical dance moves they needed to score highly.

At the 1984 Winter Olympics in Sarajevo, Bosnia, 24 million people in the UK watched them become the highest scoring figure skaters ever, when they got 12 perfect sixes from the judges for their performance to the music of Ravel's *Bolero*. The House of Commons even stopped work in the middle of a debate so the MPs could watch the

British skating legends

Two other British skaters helped make Torvill and Dean's ice-dancing success possible by getting the public to accept ice-dancing as a sport. In 1976 **JOHN CURRY** (1949–) won a gold medal for figure skating at the Olympics and brought the sport to the attention of the public. He was one of the first people to combine ballet performance with skating to create an artistic theatrical-looking routine.
In 1980 it was the turn of **ROBIN COUSINS** (1957–) to win the Olympic gold figure-skating medal and boost the interest of TV audiences.

show. That year Torvill and Dean also won the World Championship.

After their enormous Olympic success the pair turned professional and put on ice shows around the world. They competed in the Olympics once again in 1994, coming third after a controversial judging decision. In 1999 they officially retired as a team but they both work in ice-dance, coaching young dancers, helping them with dance choreography (dance routines) and producing shows. Occasionally they work together, for instance on ITV's 'Dancing on Ice' series.

DALEY THOMPSON CBE
BRITAIN'S GREATEST ALL-ROUND ATHLETE

BORN Notting Hill, London, 30 July 1958

Daley Thompson was the world's most successful decathlete, winning two Olympic gold medals in the gruelling ten-event contest.

Born of Scottish and Ugandan parents, Daley Thompson ran at school and made his decathlon debut aged 16. The decathlon is made up of ten track and field events – running races and competitions such as javelin, long-jump and shotput-throwing. It takes two days to complete and is a supreme test of an athlete's all-round skills and fitness. Each event wins an athlete a number of points towards an overall score.

Thompson appeared in his first Olympics aged 18, and although he came 18th it made him determined to succeed in the future. Four years later he won a gold medal, 150 points ahead of anybody else. In 1984 he won gold again with a world record 8,847 points. Thompson's great rival was German Jurgen Hingsen. In 1984 they battled it out for gold, and Hingsen came within 32 points of Daley's lead, but he never once managed to beat Daley during his career.

Thompson was the first athlete ever to hold Olympic, Commonwealth, European and World titles all at once. He was very strong, fast and agile and had a fierce dedication to daily training, even doing it on Christmas Day. But he managed to make the decathlon look like fun to try.

Thompson was entertaining on TV and the public loved him. But he sometimes upset people because he was seen as arrogant and didn't hold with tradition or ceremony. He famously whistled

Daley wants you

Daley Thompson's aim is to get kids all over the country involved in the 2012 Olympics, and in sport generally. He is touring the country to do just that, so look out for him visiting somewhere near you! He says his own experience of a tough childhood, and the success that sport gave him, has made him want to persuade other children to try it. If you have a sporting ambition, Daley is out to persuade you to have a go!

03'

Daley Thompson competes in the long-jump event of the decathlon during the 1984 Olympic Games.

throughout the National Anthem when he was on the medal-winning podium in 1984. By the time he retired from sport, everyone had heard of the decathlon. Since then he has featured in some popular computer games, been a fitness consultant at Chelsea Football Club and has done some television work, too. Now he is an ambassador for the 2012 London Olympics. 🇬🇧

SIR STEVE REDGRAVE CBE
BRITAIN'S GREATEST OLYMPIAN

BORN Marlow, Buckinghamshire, 23 March 1962

Steve Redgrave won five gold medals in Olympic rowing events, one of the most successful Olympians in history.

Redgrave won his unbeaten tally of golds in the Olympic Games between 1984 and 2000. He is one of only five people to win five golds or more, and one of these was his childhood hero Mark Spitz. Aged ten, Redgrave watched Spitz win seven gold medals for swimming and decided that he, too, wanted to be a champion. As he lived close to the River Thames, he decided that rowing would be his sport.

Redgrave's team

Redgrave's rowing partners were vital to his success. These included **MATTHEW PINSENT** (1970–) and **ANDY HOLMES** (1960–), **JAMES CRACKNELL** (1972–) and **TIM FOSTER** (1970–). Matthew Pinsent was also knighted and is a three-times gold medal winner. Between them, they made rowing a popular Olympic sport for the first time, and they took their place amongst our most famous living sports personalities.

Redgrave's first Olympic gold came in 1984 in the coxed fours (four people rowing together along with a rowing guide called a cox). He also won golds in the coxless pairs (two people rowing without a cox) and the coxless fours. As well as Olympic medals he won ten World Championships during his career. Most of his races were hard-fought and close – he won gold in Sydney by just 0.38 seconds. But he was more consistent than any other rower, and he had the will to put in a supreme effort at the end of a race.

After the 1996 Olympics, Redgrave famously said he would never go near a boat again, but he soon changed his mind. He even once won the World Championship for indoor rowing on a rowing machine, and was a member of the British bobsleigh team and a national bobsleigh champion!

Redgrave was lucky enough to get sponsorship so that he could devote himself full-time to the tough rowing training he had to do, getting up to row early in the morning and then working out in the gym. He said he hated the training, but did it because he wanted to win so badly. In the last four years of his rowing career he was diagnosed with colitis and diabetes, but with medical guidance and support he was able to carry on and win again. He was knighted in 2001 and since then he has raised many millions for charity, concentrating on trying to help young people. 🇬🇧

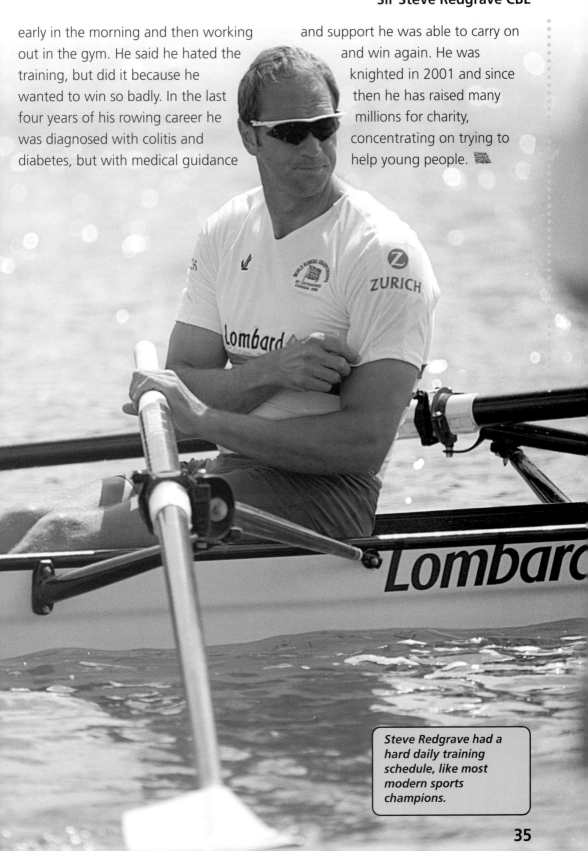

Steve Redgrave had a hard daily training schedule, like most modern sports champions.

LENNOX LEWIS CBE
WORLD HEAVYWEIGHT BOXING CHAMPION

BORN West Ham, London, 2 September 1965

Lennox Lewis is one of only three boxers in the world ever to have won the World Heavyweight Championship title three times.

Lennox was born in London to Jamaican parents. He moved to Canada when he was 12, where he excelled at all kinds of sport. His favourite was boxing, and he won the World Amateur Junior Championship when he was 17. He represented Canada in the Olympics and won gold in 1988. In the medal-winning match he knocked out future professional World Champion Riddick Bowe in the first round. Lewis moved back to Britain to turn professional, because boxing was more popular in this country than it was in Canada. He fought his way to win his first World Championship in 1993.

Lennox Lewis is tall at 195cm and has an unusually long arm reach for his height. That gives him a long punching reach which has helped him knock out many opponents. As a professional he fought 44 times and won 41 times, 32 of them by a 'KO' (knockout). This included knocking out former champion Mike Tyson in 2002. The fight against Tyson was on pay-per-view TV and made $103 million, a record for any event. Lewis' other famous fight was against Vitali Klitschko in 2003. Lewis looked as if he might lose but the referee stopped the fight after Klitschko's face got cut.

Boxing is a complicated sport and there have been various different heavyweight titles, but Lewis beat all contenders to become a true world champion. He retired in 2004, still reigning champion.

Boxing in Britain

Boxing in the UK goes back to the late 1600s. In the 18th and 19th centuries boxers often fought at fairs around the country, taking on anyone in a no-rules mix of boxing and wrestling. Boxing is split into different weight competitions (called divisions) and many Britons have succeeded in lighter categories, such as welterweight and middleweight. Lennox Lewis is one of many British boxing stars to have fought on the world stage.

Lennox is a quiet calm person who did not generate the publicity surrounding more notorious boxers, such as Tyson. Since he stopped boxing he has commentated and appeared in the film *Ocean's Eleven*, shown fighting his big adversary Klitschko. He still appears in TV adverts as a well-known and well-loved British sporting star.

Lennox Lewis carries his World Championship belts, the top prize in boxing,

DAME TANNI GREY-THOMPSON

BRITAIN'S GREATEST PARALYMPIC ATHLETE

BORN Cardiff, Wales, 26 July 1969

Britain's most successful disabled athlete, Tanni Grey-Thompson, has won an incredible 11 Paralympic gold medals.

Born with the medical condition spina bifida, Tanni was forced to use a wheelchair from the age of seven. As a child, she loved sport, and her hero was Welsh rugby hero Gareth Edwards (see pages 22–23).

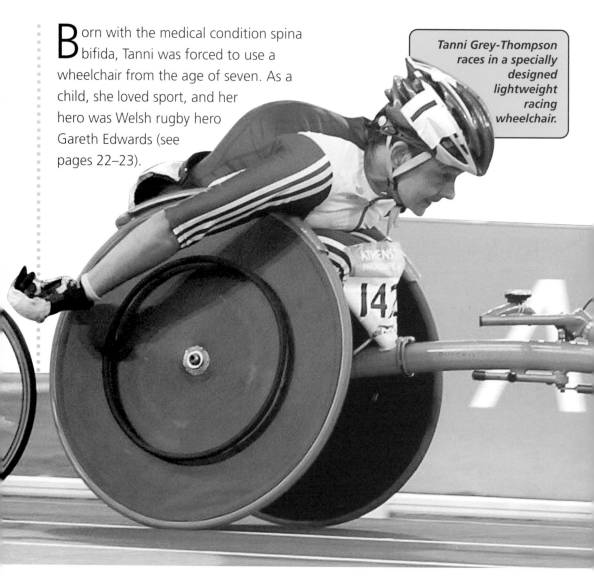

Tanni Grey-Thompson races in a specially designed lightweight racing wheelchair.

While she was still at school she began to compete in wheelchair athletics, and represented Wales when she was 15. She won her first Paralympic medal in 1988. From then on she bagged medal after medal in every Paralympics up to 2004. She won her 11 golds in the 100m, 200m, 400m and 800m track races, using a lightweight racing chair and powering it with her arms.

Tanni's Olympic wheelchair training was a tough regime of 160km a week. In addition she has won six London Marathons in the wheelchair part of the event. In 2002 she won it just three months after giving birth to her daughter. Overall she has won 16 Paralympic medals, and held 30 world records.

Paralympic success

The Paralympic Games are held every four years, after the Olympic Games. Athletes with disabilities can enter the various track and field events, plus swimming and team events such as football and rugby. At the Winter Paralympics, disabled sportspeople compete in such sports as skiing, curling and ice sledge hockey. Apart from Tanni, other successful British Paralympians include horseman, **LEE PEARSON** (1974–), and swimmers **DAVE ROBERTS** (1980–) and **JIM ANDERSON** (1963–).

Tanni's success has made her one of the most well-known women athletes in the country, and she has also brought lots of welcome attention for Paralympic sport. Now she advises young Paralympians hoping to match her achievements. She was made a Dame for her overall contribution to British sport.

Tanni's career has proved inspiring to many people, both disabled and able-bodied. The publicity surrounding her wins has helped boost disabled sport in the UK. Tanni is now retired but works to promote sport for all, and helped with Britain's successful 2012 Olympic bid.

DAME KELLY HOLMES
DOUBLE GOLD MEDAL-WINNING RUNNER

BORN Pembury, Kent, 19 April 1970

Kelly Holmes battled through a career dogged by injury to achieve her dream – two gold medals in the 2004 Olympics, for the 800m and 1500m middle-distance races.

When Kelly was 12 she joined a local athletics club and soon she won the English Schools 1500m title. Her childhood hero was Sebastian Coe, legendary British middle-distance runner (see page 12). In those days there were no grants from the Lottery Fund to help athletes financially, and so it was very difficult to concentrate on training full-time. For a while Kelly gave up athletics and joined the army instead. She was an army lorry-driver and then a physical training instructor, reaching the rank of Sergeant. She won many army athletics events, and became army judo champion, too. Eventually she got funding to help try again for a career as a full-time athlete. Kelly won Commonwealth gold in 1994 but world success was slow coming. She was unlucky with injuries, often suffering them before big events. In 2000 she won bronze at the Olympics, and then moved to Africa to train with her great friend and rival Maria Mutola of Mozambique. Early training for the 2004 Olympics did not go well and she suffered more leg injuries. At that difficult time she was diagnosed with depression, and she has since talked about how she felt and how she managed to come through it.

Olympic arguing

To compete in the Olympics, athletes must be amateur. But the rules have altered over the years and now athletes can earn extra money from such sources as sponsorship deals, books and the Lottery Fund. They just do not get paid for appearing in the Olympics themselves. These rules have changed gradually, after lots of controversy and rows, and now money is less of a big issue. Instead illegal performance-enhancing drugs provide the Olympic controversy, with athletes being thrown out of the competition if they fail official drug tests.

She hopes that her experience and eventual success will help and inspire other people to cope with depression. At last Kelly reached the 2004 Olympics injury-free, and powered twice through the opposition to win two triumphant gold medals. She finally got her reward for the many hours of training and what she called 'twenty years of dreaming'. Her great hero, Sebastian Coe, presented her with a medal, and 40,000 people lined the streets to welcome her back to her home town of Tonbridge. She retired in 2005, knowing it was impossible to top her 2004 achievement.

Kelly Holmes acknowledges the cheers of the crowd. She is a successful and very popular British Olympian.

DAVID BECKHAM OBE
FOOTBALLING SUPERSTAR

BORN Leytonstone, London, 2 May 1975

David Beckham is a footballing superstar, known worldwide as much for his filmstar lifestyle as his midfield skills. He captained England from 2000 to 2006, and won honours with Manchester United.

As a child, Beckham played in a football team coached by his dad, and also went to a football training school in Manchester run by World Cup-winner Bobby Charlton. He joined Manchester United Football Club as a youth player and made it into their first team when he was 17. While he was there he helped win many team honours, including the Treble in 1999 (League, FA Cup and EUFA Champions League titles). He moved to Real Madrid, a Spanish football team, in 2003 and in 2007 agreed a record-breaking $250 million contract with US team Los Angeles Galaxy, making him the highest-paid US sportsman. Beckham, famously nicknamed 'Becks', is the only Englishman to have scored in three different World Cups. He scored two of these from direct free kicks, his trademark. The title of the film *Bend it like Beckham* referred to his amazing ability to curl the ball accurately into the net from a free kick. He practised this move every day, kicking ball after ball onto a target. Like Ian Botham (see pages 26–27), his refusal to give up often lifted his team from likely defeat to eventual victory.

Even stars practise (and they don't eat junk)

Football is a game that everyone can try, but to get better and to stay successful takes practice and even stars such as David Beckham and **WAYNE ROONEY** (1985–) train with their team and on their own, practising shots every day. They have carefully planned training schedules, fitness regimes and they must monitor what they eat if they want to stay at their peak. Take inspiration from the stars by eating healthily and doing some regular exercise. If you decide to try a sport, its worth giving yourself some practice time, too.

David Beckham wears the England football strip. His image has made him a fortune.

But things have not always gone well for Becks. As a young World Cup player in 1998 he was blamed for England being knocked out, after he was sent off for kicking out at another player. For a while he was England's most hated player, yet he has become England's most famous player. He is, however, the first England Captain ever to be sent off, and the first England player ever to be sent off twice. When Beckham married Victoria Adams, a former member of The Spice Girls pop group, he became a global celebrity. He hit the headlines every day for what he wore and which celebrities were his friends. His fame helped him to earn a great deal of money from endorsing (advertising) products around the world. In 2002 he became the highest-earning footballer in the world. He runs football academies in the USA and wants to promote soccer there. He is also a goodwill ambassador for UNICEF, using his fame to help UNICEF's charity work.

DAME ELLEN MacARTHUR
RECORD-BREAKING SAILOR

BORN Derbyshire,
8 July 1976

Ellen MacArthur is Britain's most successful sailor. In 2005 she smashed the world record for the fastest non-stop single-handed trip around the world.

When Ellen was four she began to go sailing with her aunt, and instantly loved it. When she was eight she began to save her dinner money to buy herself a boat. She finally got her first dinghy when she was 13. When she was 18, Ellen went into full-time yachting, working on a boat and teaching sailing. A year later she sailed single-handedly around Britain. In 2001 she came second in the gruelling Vendée Globe solo round-the-world race, becoming the youngest person and the fastest woman ever to sail around the world alone, even though she changed course during the race to help a fellow sailor out of trouble.

By now Ellen was able to get a sponsor, the Kingfisher Company, to help pay for her boats. It cost over £2 million to build a round-the-world racing yacht, and run the backup team needed to help with the race, so sponsorship was essential. Ellen achieved her 2004/5 record in a specially-built trimaran, which has three hulls side-by-side. She is only 1.57m tall, so everything in her boat was designed for her small height. Between the three hulls there was a 'deck' of netting that was bouncy like a trampoline. Occasionally Ellen had to climb the 90m-high mast to do repairs, even in stormy

Talking to Ellen

Ellen is able to make use of modern technology on her solo voyages. She can talk to her team back home via satellite phone, and use satellite navigation, too. She also makes regular updates to her website as she sails, and her fans can send her encouraging messages via the Internet. However, even with all this technology, it is her personal strength of character that counts, and when she gets back home from a race she does what all top sportspeople do... She starts to train for the next one!

weather. The cockpit was a small slot about 4.7m long, and down below there was a very small living space with a bunk, sink, stove and map table.

Washing had to be done with a bucket, and meals were freeze-dried food mixed with water. Ellen could only sleep in 15-minute catnaps, because she had to be alert and ready to adjust sail ropes or do running repairs on a boat going so fast it sometimes felt, she said, like a 'Tube train out of control'.

Ellen began her world-record attempt in November 2004 and sailed non-stop to the finish line in February, 2005, taking just over 71 days and knocking nearly a day-and-a-half off the existing record. On her triumphant return she was knighted, and took another record by becoming Britain's youngest ever Dame! She continues to race, sometimes solo and sometimes as a team Captain, and continues to break records. She has outstanding mental toughness, determination and fearlessness, truly one of the greatest British sportspeople ever.

Ellen MacArthur is an example of someone totally dedicated to their chosen sport.

GLOSSARY

All Blacks The New Zealand international rugby team, who play in an all-black strip.

Amateur Someone who does not earn money from taking part in a sports event.

Ashes The name for the Test match series played between Australia and England.

Barbarians An international rugby team of players from different nations.

British Lions An international touring rugby team made up of players from England, Scotland, Wales and Ireland.

Choreography A series of carefully worked out moves used in an ice-dancing routine or other dance piece.

Coach Someone who trains sportspeople.

Commonwealth Games An event held for athletes from the Commonwealth – Britain and a group of countries once ruled by Britain.

Contract A legal agreement. A professional footballer has a contract with his team, setting out details such as wages.

Debut A first appearance in a sporting event, such as the first time a footballer plays for a new team.

Decathlon An Olympic event made up of ten different sports.

Double century Two hundred runs scored in one cricket innings.

Endorsement Allowing your name to be used to advertise a product, such as a footballer advertising football boots.

Fielder A cricket player positioned in the field ready to stop or to catch a ball.

First class runs Cricket runs scored in international cricket matches or top club cricket.

Grand Prix A top class international event in motorsports, such as Formula One racing and Superbikes.

Grand Slam A term used in rugby to mean beating every other team in the 'Six Nations' competition.

Heavyweight boxing Fights held between boxers weighing 200lb and above.

Home nations England, Scotland, Wales and Ireland. A term used in rugby.

International Someone who plays for their country.

Knighthood An honour granted by the reigning monarch, giving the title 'Sir' or 'Dame'.

KO When a boxer gets knocked out in a boxing ring, losing the fight.

Lottery Funding Money granted from the National Lottery, sometimes given to sportspeople to help them train full-time.

Middle-distance races 800m, 1500m and 3000m athletics races.

Olympian Someone who has won a medal at an Olympic games.

Olympics An international sports event held every four years, made up of many different sports. The Summer Olympic Games include athletics, swimming and many other sports. The Winter Olympic Games include winter sports, such as skiing and skating.

Pacemaker Someone who runs fast in one stretch of an athletics race, to help a fellow athlete to make a good overall time (they do this by keeping up with the pacemaker and then running on to victory).

Paralympics The Olympic Games held specifically for sportspeople with disabilities.

Performance-enhancing drugs Drugs that give an athlete a better performance by making them faster or stronger than they would normally be.

Professional Someone who makes their living from playing sport.

Record A sporting achievement such as a winning time or score that nobody else has achieved.

Referee The chief sports official who enforces the rules in sports such as football and rugby.

Ryder Cup A golf competition played every two years between Europe and the USA.

Scout Someone who is a talent-spotter for a sports team, such as a professional football or cricket team.

Single-handed A term in sailing meaning that one person is sailing a boat.

Sponsorship Financial support given from a company to an athlete, in return for them giving the company publicity such as wearing their logo on equipment or sports clothing.

Sports psychology The study of how sportspeople can prepare mentally to help themselves perform better.

Test match A match between two international teams in sports such as cricket and rugby.

Test player Someone playing in an international cricket match.

Treble Three important football honours won in the same year – usually referring to the Premier League title, the FA Cup title and the EUFA Champions League title.

Trimaran A boat with three long narrow hulls, side-by-side.

Triple Crown The honour of beating three other home nations in a rugby competition held yearly.

Umpire The name for a referee in some sports, such as cricket and tennis.

World Cup International football competition played every four years.

SOME PLACES TO VISIT

All over the country there are places where you can try out new sports. Find out how to get involved at your local sports centre. For a list of sports museums around the country go to www.sportsmuseums.co.uk.

Brooklands Museum, Surrey
See the oldest ever purpose-built motor-racing track.

Football Museums
There are football museums in the grounds of several big British clubs.

The MCC Museum, Lords Cricket Ground, London
The oldest sports museum in the world, this is dedicated to cricket.

Museum of Rugby, Twickenham, London
Home of English rugby.

National Football Museum, Preston North End football ground
Find out how football began.

National Motorcycle Museum, Birmingham
See more than 650 motorcycles.

Scottish Football Museum, Glasgow
Find out about Scottish football.

Wimbledon Lawn Tennis Museum, Wimbledon, London
A museum dedicated to tennis.

Some useful websites

www.bbc.co.uk/cbbc/sport/index.shtml
Find out about sports stars, tricks and tips and all kinds of entertaining sports facts.

www.exploratorium.edu/sports/
Lots of amazing sports science, such as how to improve your skateboarding and ball throwing the scientific way.

www.guinnessworldrecords.com
Find a world record, watch videos of record-breaking attempts and find out how to break a record yourself!

Note to parents and teachers:
Every effort has been made by the Publishers to ensure that the websites in this book are suitable for children, that they are of the highest educational value, and that they contain no inappropriate or offensive material. However, because of the nature of the Internet, it is impossible to guarantee that the contents of these sites will not be altered. We strongly advise that Internet access is supervised by a responsible adult.

Index

These are the lists of contents for each title in *Great Britons*:

LEADERS
Boudica • Alfred the Great • Richard I • Edward I • Robert Bruce
Owain Glyndwr • Henry V • Henry VIII • Elizabeth I
Oliver Cromwell • The Duke of Marlborough • Robert Walpole
Horatio Nelson • Queen Victoria • Benjamin Disraeli
William Gladstone • David Lloyd George • Winston Churchill
Clement Attlee • Margaret Thatcher

CAMPAIGNERS FOR CHANGE
John Wycliffe • John Lilburne • Thomas Paine • Mary Wollstonecraft
William Wilberforce • Elizabeth Fry • William Lovett
Edwin Chadwick • Lord Shaftesbury • Florence Nightingale
Josephine Butler • Annie Besant • James Keir Hardie • Emmeline Pankhurst
Eleanor Rathbone • Ellen Wilkinson • Lord David Pitt • Bruce Kent
Jonathon Porritt • Shami Chakrabati

NOVELISTS
Aphra Behn • Jonathan Swift • Henry Fielding • Jane Austen
Charles Dickens • The Brontë Sisters • George Eliot • Lewis Carroll
Thomas Hardy • Robert Louis Stevenson • Arthur Conan Doyle
Virginia Woolf • D H Lawrence • J R R Tolkien • George Orwell
Graham Greene • William Golding • Ian McEwan • J K Rowling
Caryl Phillips • Andrea Levy • Zadie Smith
Monica Ali • Salman Rushdie

ARTISTS
Nicholas Hilliard • James Thornhill • William Hogarth
Joshua Reynolds • George Stubbs • William Blake • J M W Turner
John Constable • David Wilkie • Dante Gabriel Rossetti
Walter Sickert • Gwen John • Wyndham Lewis • Vanessa Bell
Henry Moore • Barbara Hepworth • Francis Bacon • David Hockney
Anish Kapoor • Damien Hirst

ENGINEERS
Robert Hooke • Abraham Darby • James Watt • John MacAdam
Thomas Telford • George Cayley • George Stephenson • Robert Stephenson
Joseph Paxton • Isambard Kingdom Brunel • Henry Bessemer
Joseph Bazalgette • Joseph Whitworth • Charles Parsons • Henry Royce
Nigel Gresley • Lord Nuffield • Harry Ricardo • Frank Whittle • Norman Foster

SCIENTISTS
John Dee • Robert Boyle • Isaac Newton • Edmond Halley • William Herschel
Michael Faraday • Charles Babbage • Mary Anning • Charles Darwin
Lord Kelvin • James Clerk Maxwell • Ernest Rutherford • Joseph Rotblat
Dorothy Hodgkin • Alan Turing • Francis Crick • Stephen Hawking
John Sulston • Jocelyn Bell Burnell • Susan Greenfield

SPORTING HEROES
WG Grace • Arthur Wharton • Kitty Godfree • Roger Bannister
Stirling Moss • Jackie Stewart • Bobby Moore • George Best
Gareth Edwards • Barry Sheene • Ian Botham • Nick Faldo
Torville and Dean • Lennox Lewis • Daley Thompson • Steve Redgrave
Tanni Grey-Thompson • Kelly Holmes • David Beckham • Ellen McArthur

MUSICIANS
William Byrd • Henry Purcell • George Frideric Handel • Arthur Sullivan
Edward Elgar • Henry Wood • Ralph Vaughan Williams • Noel Coward
Michael Tippet • Benjamin Britten • Vera Lynn
John Dankworth and Cleo Laine • Jacqueline Du Pre
Eric Clapton • Andrew Lloyd Webber • Elvis Costello
Simon Rattle • The Beatles • Courtney Pine • Evelyn Glennie